TRUE TEAM

SARAH SINGER-NOURIE

RIPPLE
PRESS

Cincinnati, Ohio

This publication is designed to provide competent and reliable information regarding the subject matter covered. However, it is sold with the understanding that the author and publisher are not engaged in rendering legal, financial, or other professional advice. Laws and practices often vary from state to state and country to country, and if legal or other expert assistance is required, the services of a professional should be sought. The author and publisher specifically disclaim any liability that is incurred from the use or application of the contents of this book.

Published by Ripple Press

Ripple Press
10411 Shadyside Lane
Cincinnati, OH 45249

ISBN: 979-8-9904135-0-4 (paperback)
ISBN: 979-8-9904135-1-1 (ebook)
LCCN 2024910849

Printed in the United States of America

DEDICATION

For Sarah, your immeasurable impact,
boundless love, and relentless commitment to
leave the world a better place will fuel us
the rest of our lives.

TABLE OF CONTENTS

Foreword   by Blair Singer — 1

Chapter 0:   **No More Secrets & Magic** — 5

Chapter 0.9: **Just in Time** — 9

Chapter 1:   **Safety First:** How to See the #1 Determiner of
Team Invisibly at Play Right Now — 13

Chapter 2:   **Agree to Agree:** How to Set Agreements
That Accelerate Progress and Make
Accountability Easy — 19

Chapter 3:   **Call It, Own It, Move On:** How to Call Things Out
Easily Without Drama — 25

Chapter 4:   **Confront or Avoid?** How to See and Adapt Your
Conflict Style Within the Team — 31

Chapter 5:   **Checking In:** How to Keep the Most Important
Communication Flowing — 37

Chapter 6:   **Step Out:** How to Get Everyone Out of the
Comfort Zone and Be Okay With It — 47

Chapter 7:   **Get It:** How to Make Learning Easier & Keep
Pushing Until It's Solid — 53

Chapter 8: **Get "Reality":** How to Reframe Anything That Happens to Keep the Outlook Healthy — 59

Chapter 9: **Upsets Happen:** How to Dismantle Any Agitation Into a Solvable Problem — 65

Chapter 10: **IN-10-TION:** How to Get Judgment Out of the Way of Greatness — 69

Chapter 11: **Spark Motivation:** How to Get Out of Your World and Make it Matter in Theirs (Owning It) — 75

Chapter 12: **Above the Line:** Responding in a Way That's Open, Frank, and Conscientious — 81

Chapter 13: **State:** How to Spark, Set, and Change Energy on the Spot — 85

Chapter 14: **Be It. Do It. Have It.** How to Make True Impact Every Time While Expanding Your Range — 91

Chapter 15: **Get Perspective:** Leveraging the Pyramid of Perspective — 99

Chapter 16: **Perturbation:** Managing the Pressure of Transformation — 105

Chapter 17: **The C-Chair of Trust:** How to Quickly Build and Repair Trust Without Drama — 111

Chapter 18: **Feedback, for the Win:** How to Deliver It, How to Hear It — 117

A Little About Me — 125

FOREWORD

One of the greatest assets that any organization can have is a great team. Yet in many cases, their team is either non-performing or a downright liability. What determines the value of the team seems independent of the individuals, the tasks, or even the talent. We think of great teams in their moments of brilliance in sports, in business, in families, in battles, and in cultures. Thousands of books and case studies have attempted to isolate the exact ingredients and recipes for taking regular people and turning them into championship teams.

Why? Because there's so much at stake. We know that to scale any business requires a team. Families are teams. Our communities are teams. Our customers are teams. We know that life is lived in groups, tribes, and teams. Yet the world we live in seems polarized. Right versus left, gender versus gender, east versus west, etc. As the population of our planet surpasses eight billion, we find ourselves challenged to find a formula that allows us to work together in our respective genius, creating the magic that can only be accomplished by a great team.

Few people have cracked this code, probably because they were looking at it from the wrong perspective. In thirty years of training and coaching, I know that if you assume the student is smart...they will turn out to be brilliant. Yet if you assume they're going to be a problem, you'll be right as well. In her book *Tap Into Greatness*, Sarah Singer assumed that greatness is inherent in everyone. Looking for that greatness revealed magic. As a result, some of the most powerful corporate executives and coaches across America cherished their team's interactions with Sarah as she continually found the gems of greatness in all the individuals and leaders she coached.

You see, Sarah was my sister, and she always saw the light in everyone. We used to tease her that she was naïve and would have to learn life the hard way. As she grew and became an amazing teacher of young children and teenagers, her magic touch continued to develop. She wasn't naïve — she saw something that most people either just give lip service to or don't see at all. She used to say that every child who walked into her classes had a Post-It note on their forehead with a number from one to ten. She said she literally hung a ten on every child regardless of what was already there. Her results in even the most difficult situations were legendary. Her understanding of how the brain works, how human behavior can shift in an instant, and how to mine the greatness in each child, team member, and individual became her passion, her reputation, and her legacy.

A horrible and incurable brain tumor snatched Sarah away from us, but her teachings and the lives she transformed remained. This book, "True Teams," was the last book she wrote as the cancer did its deadly work. She had found the "secret sauce," and it was a quantum leap. It was simple, elegant, and profound. Her desire for this world was to do whatever she could to make it work. She came into this world with that belief, and wherever she is now, I'm sure she is still trying to make it work.

The wisdom in these pages is only for those who believe we can be great as parents, leaders, coaches, teachers, friends, and human beings. Not perfect, not without emotion, not soft, but certainly honest. In a world where people seem to be at each other's throats at a greater and greater intensity, Sarah's is a process that is a true light in the eye of a storm. Experience its power, its warmth, its strength, and its love. It is Sarah's greatest gift to you and those you spend your life with.

—**Blair Singer,** *founder Blair Singer Training Academy, author and brother*

0.

NO MORE
SECRETS & MAGIC

What *if you could get any team to a level of complete trust, self-sustaining energy, drama-free focus, standard-pushing performance, generative collaboration, and fast learning?*

What if they could harness their talent and motivation on demand, solve conflicts quickly, give and get direct feedback easily, and get to an optimal mindset any time?

What if that elusive team "magic" or "secret sauce" were easy, buildable, and possible for your team right now?

Spoiler: It's completely possible.

Yet I've resisted writing this book for a long time. When asked in the past if there was a "quick-guide version of team-building" for me to just hand over to people rather than taking them through a process, my response always was "No, and even if there were, I wouldn't give it to you, because you *need to go through* the whole process and the deep work that gets a group to become a true team."

Now I see it differently. I love that deep work; it powerfully opens up a rarefied level of trust and capacity on a team, and I love facilitating it. Yet it's also not the *only* way to get a team set, strong, accelerating, optimally performing, and building forward.

Until now, there hasn't yet been a sound, effective, agreed-upon method for this. We also haven't even had a good way to describe it, so we've been left with using mysterious descriptors, like a team either "having that magic" or "secret sauce" or not.

Luckily, it's *not* magic, and it doesn't need to be a secret. People once called phenomena such as gravity "magic" until we actually learned the science of it. Now, it's time to demystify the magic of "team," too. You're about to find that it's simpler and faster than you think.

In my decades of coaching leaders and teams to break through to another level, I've discovered the specific behaviors, conditions, interactions, reframes, and tools that consistently build and accelerate teams. There's a growing body of research that explains why these work: They're learnable, repeatable, powerful, and scalable. You can use this toolkit and process with your own style.

Think of it like a high-performance racing bike: If I realize there's a loose gear that, if tightened, will get me better/faster/smoother performance, I need the right wrench for it. A hammer might be nearby, but that isn't helpful, even when combined with my bike IQ, mechanical intuition, and repair savvy. It's just the wrong tool and will cause damage rather than improve anything. Yet if I leave that loose gear alone, the bike won't improve itself and it'll definitely get worse.

Your team is just like that.

They need the right tools to tighten specific human gears at the right time to get to their next level of performance. Just doing what they do together (playing the game, doing the work, etc.) won't take care of those specific "loose gear" issues. The tools you have and default to currently as the team manager might be familiar, yet they might not be especially effective or powerful, and are possibly even doing more damage than good.

You've hired talented people with great intentions, yet you know they could be better. So do I. That's why we're here.

In the following pages, you'll learn the precise tools that will transform your team into what is possible every time.

I've coached pharmaceutical teams, engineering teams, sports teams, educational teams (both teachers and students), strategy teams, design teams, marketing teams, accounting teams, media teams, research teams, analysis teams, medical teams, distribution line teams, hairstyling teams, religious teams, manufacturing teams, community volunteering teams, restaurant teams, kitchen teams, retail teams, camp facilitator teams, executive teams, remote teams, cross-functional teams, startup teams, nonprofit teams, positive teams, negative teams, functional teams, and dysfunctional teams...*and I've tested these tools with every one of them to get this down to the right set of tools that work best.* This is it — the ultimate True Team kit.

**If you're one of those coaches or leaders who swears by your own "magic," thank you for being here. We're about to name and describe repeatable, teachable steps, some of which you may have already been doing intuitively, and upgrade it all to more, faster, better steps.

"A team is not a group of people that work together. A team is a group of people that trust each other."

–Simon Sinek

0.9

JUST IN TIME

A Division I Basketball coach recently texted me with a question. "Can you tell me that one thing again about how to quickly get trust on the team?" he asked. He was referencing a conversation we'd had a few weeks prior in which I'd explained how to do this, yet he wasn't really taking it in because he didn't think he needed it at the time. So, his text meant things had shifted for him. He was experiencing a moment of frustration — of what wasn't working to build trust on the team — and he needed the answer. So I gave it to him again, this time just in time.

You've likely done the same thing: You've read about or heard or been told something that someone else thought was a good idea, maybe even what someone else thought was "essential" for you, but it went in one ear and out the other, right? Later, you may have had that moment when you actually needed to remember that thing and thought, "Wait...*what* was it that they told me?"

This is perfectly normal. That basketball coach (and you in those instances) didn't really hear it the first time or remember that idea later, because your brain simply didn't think it was essential at the time...it wasn't primed to learn *that* thing in *that* moment.

The stickiest kind of learning there is — the kind that actually sticks in your brain — happens *just in time* when we're in the moment of question or challenge and the answer just appears. It can feel like an a-ha moment...like the universe aligning into perfect sense for that moment.

This is why my favorite kind of coaching is *just-in-time* live coaching — when I'm actually *on* the court *with* you, seeing the problem you can't or the easier/faster/more effective way to do what you're working too hard to do, and I give it to you right there in the moment, making it instantly effective. *That's* just-in-time learning.

And *this* is your just-in-time guidebook, that secret sauce broken down into the Team frameworks and tools you need that you can access exactly when you need them. Like spotting a loose gear that's making your high-performance bike wobble and having the perfect-sized Allen wrench magically materialize in your hand to fix it, this book will provide those perfect tools for you, on demand.

I'll give them to you one by one (each microchapter is its own tool), so you'll have them within reach all the time.

HOW TO USE & PRIME THIS BOOK

1. **Big Picture.** You can skim or even read this whole book in one sitting, right now, and you'll get it all in concept, seeing how the pieces relate and influence one another like dominoes.
2. **Chunks.** Read a section, think about it, maybe try it out, then read, think, try another, and repeat.

3. **Just in Time.** Once you've read and completed the tasks in the first chapter, you can pull/practice the right tools, at the right time, from all over this book. (You might want to get a few copies — one that lives on top of your desk, one in the team meeting room, one on your bedside table, etc.)

Whether you're currently leading or coaching a team, a member of a team, or getting ready to build a new team, you're in the right place.

Your team is primed, but deep down, they know they could be better.

So now, let's get them there.

"You do your
best work when
you feel safe."

–Julianna Margulies

1.

SAFETY FIRST

HOW TO SEE THE #1 DETERMINER OF TEAM INVISIBLY AT PLAY RIGHT NOW

When you need this:

- As a new team begins working together
- Before anything else, yet especially when the pressure hits
- If the team falls into patterns of holding back or shutting down

Why you need this:

Unfortunately, statistics tell us that you've likely experienced a situation (a job, team, or relationship) in which it wasn't okay to make a mistake, share a wacky idea, or push back... where you had to first weigh the cost of doing so, ranging from slight discomfort to possible retaliation or punishment. You've likely also seen teams in which the ingredients all seemed right — awesome talent, motivated, and solidly confident stars — yet their output was mediocre, and people didn't speak up, take risks, or play full out. These are common issues that are frustrating, yet fixable!

According to a recent study by the U.S. National Institutes of Health, **psychological safety is the single most important determiner of team performance**. It's bigger than talent, bigger than personality, and bigger than potential. It's what *has* to be in place for teams to accelerate or perform to the level they're truly able to. Full stop.

UNDERSTAND:

Psychological safety is a working climate in which people feel comfortable to speak up, question, express themselves, push back, take a risk, or admit error without negative repercussions.

The most unnerving part of this is that when people *don't* feel psychologically safe, it won't be brought forward — people stay *silent*.

Findings show that psychological safety is even necessary for the most confident and accomplished performers to be able to play full out, yet it's not something most of us even consciously realize.

Consider how it plays out on your team: When someone makes a mistake, speaks up, or pushes back, what happens? If you're the leader, how do you react?

If you (or the team) slams them or shuts them down in any of these ways, you're destroying psychological safety:

- **Shame.** Saying "You are _____" (insert negative character trait like "bad," "stupid," "dishonest," "a liar," "an idiot," etc).
- **Insult.** Snapping back at them about their character or who they are, making it personal.

- **Threat.** Insinuating that there will be negative repercussions if they continue further or do this again, including sarcastic or passive-aggressive threats veiled as "joking."
- **Humiliate.** Ridiculing, belittling, or making fun of someone or their ideas; publicly blaming the problem or failure of something on someone.
- **Silence or dismissive.** Shutting them down, justifying or minimizing what they're speaking up about, or disregarding or not acknowledging what they're trying to say.
- **Punish.** Taking corrective action or revoking or blocking their access or opportunities without proper process.

When experiencing any of the situations described above, our self-protective brains learn a powerful thing: Do not put yourself in that position again. This leads people, even the stars on your team, to play it safe, stay small, hide mistakes, and withhold ideas (even the game-changing ones) for the sake of saving face and embarrassment.

In the *Bad Apple Effect*, author T. Mitchell Felps notes that even one toxic person on a team can compromise psychological safety to the point of decreasing the whole team's performance by as much as forty percent.

This doesn't mean you can't push people hard or hold people accountable. You can and should do that in a true team, yet it will only work to improve performance if people feel safe, not threatened.

The good news: You can build psychological safety! It's actually pretty simple to do, and once you get going, it accelerates everything else!

START:

- **Replace behaviors and language that destroy psychological safety (see the list above).** If you're the team leader, this is crucial, as nothing else will shift until you do. You can maintain intensity and toughness, yet still keep your actions and words psychologically safe.

- **Listen and acknowledge.** Instead of defending or shutting down when people speak up, listen to them and acknowledge what they're saying. You don't have to agree or disagree — just acknowledge (repeat it back) and thank them for their candor.

- **Reframe failure.** Nobody wants to fail — they want to get better. But failure is a natural part of the learning/experimenting process, so frame it that way. Acknowledge the sting of failure, then quickly move to what's possible to learn from it. Having a "no failures" goal is a setup for people to hide and/or increase their mistakes. A better goal is faster learning!

- **Create team agreements**. People need to know *what* they can count on from others, or they hold back and won't trust. (We'll cover this more in chapter 3.)

- **Celebrate learnings, even if they're failures.** Practice calling out and celebrating personal and team learnings! In a study done some years ago, researchers found that the more experience people get safely admitting an error or failure and associating positive growth from it, the more they'll speak up and also make fewer mistakes.

- **Stop-Start-Continue feedback.** Check in with another person one on one, and take turns telling one another 1) something you'd like me to stop doing, 2) something you'd like me to start doing, and 3) something you'd like me to continue doing.

- **Implement a "no zinger" policy.** Zingers are sarcastic comments that insult through the use of a joke — a passive-aggressive way to belittle or embarrass. Zingers force people to stay emotionally on guard, killing innovation and creativity. Anything that you might follow with a "Just kidding" comment is a zinger.

- **Consider the 2x2.** The tool outlined in the illustration below, which is from Amy Edmondson's book, *The Fearless Organization,* can be tricky to use, because if psychological safety is low, people won't want to speak up about it, so a discussion about this on the team might give you a false read. But it can also be highly effective if used correctly. Have teammates consider it, keep using the tools, and revisit this to assess:
    - Which quadrant are we each in?
    - Which quadrant is our team operating in?
    - What needs to start, stop, or continue in order to get to that upper right quadrant?
    - What agreements could get us there?

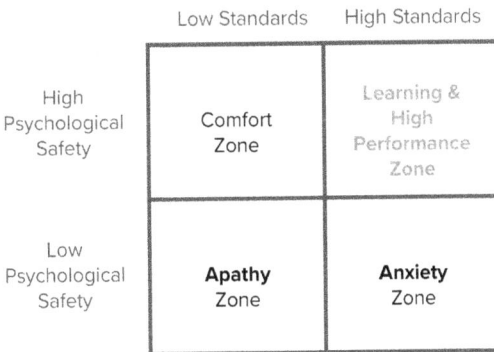

	Low Standards	High Standards
High Psychological Safety	Comfort Zone	Learning & High Performance Zone
Low Psychological Safety	Apathy Zone	Anxiety Zone

From: Amy Edmondson, *The Fearless Organization.* 2019, Wiley "

"Coming together
is a beginning.
Keeping together
is progress.
Working together
is success."

–Henry Ford

2.

AGREE TO AGREE

HOW TO SET AGREEMENTS THAT ACCELERATE PROGRESS AND MAKE ACCOUNTABILITY EASY

When your team needs this:

- As a new team begins working together
- Before the pressure hits (because you really need it in place when the pressure hits)
- As you fall into your normal patterns, which might not be helping the team

Why your team needs this:

The best teams tend to outperform the sum of their individual players' talent and achieve an exceptional level of performance when they truly come together to fully trust one another, play all-in, and bring their absolute best, 100% effort. They also tend to get better in crunch time, because they're already counting on one another, so they lean in to focus and tap into that collective energy even more...

That's because they know and trust exactly what they can expect from every other person, no matter what, because they've set it and agreed to it from the beginning. While some teams figure this out over time, the most efficient teams get it set right out of the gate, check in about it often, and tweak it as needed.

UNDERSTAND:

- It's tough to fully trust or play full out for a team until you know what you can count on without question from your teammates.

- It's easy to hold someone accountable to an agreement they've made. It's hard to hold them accountable to an expectation you have but that they haven't agreed to.

- Agreements free up energy (the energy that's currently being spent guessing and doing risk assessment) to accelerate forward, play full out at 100%, and not worry about whether or not teammates will do their part.

- According to Project Aristotle, the most solid, high-performing teams have a context of team rules and agreements and follow a consistent behavior of keeping agreements with one another, which holds them together and accountable to each other. (Source: Project Aristotle)

- Agreements help create trust, psychological safety, and the solidity of what everyone can both count on and hold one another to. They keep everyone playing in sync.

- The more individually talented and innovative you and your teammates are, the more diversity of thought, style, standards, and expectations are at play. You need agreement on how you'll work together to create space for that diversity to come through as an advantage that expands your team's capacity.

- If you don't have an agreement in place, you're left to just give an opinion, such as "I like it" or "I don't like it" or "I approve" or "I don't approve" or "You're too X," which is too subjective, not scalable, and ultimately just your opinion vs. theirs. The person you're speaking to can too quickly go into denial mode. So instead...

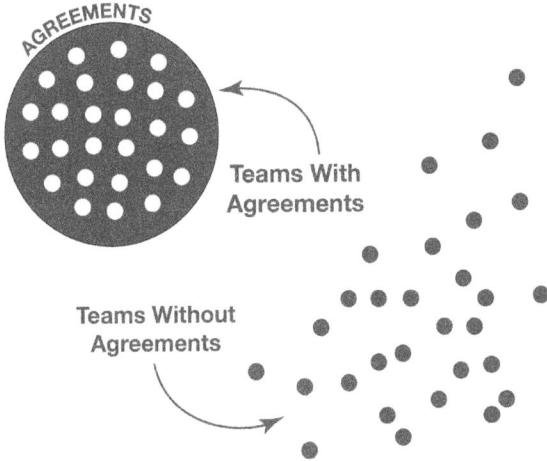

AGREEMENTS

Teams With
Agreements

Teams Without
Agreements

HOW:

- **Huddle the whole team.** Agreements work when people create them together. Rules created and enforced by leaders are very different from a pact of agreements the team creates themselves. We automatically own what we create, so have the team create the necessary agreements.

- **Tell the why.** Establish context. For instance, you might say, "We're creating our own set of team agreements, so we can all know exactly what we can count on from one another every day."

- **Brainstorm a list of the behaviors and patterns** that get in the way of being able to trust, accelerate with one another. Use the post-it-bs method on page 2 to create your list.
  - Ask: What team or teammate behaviors have gotten in the way in the past or with other teams you've been on? You're looking for the things that cause you to hold back and not want to play full out.
  - Example: When someone makes a decision that affects everyone without checking in with the team first

- **Brainstorm simple agreements** that would prevent those unhealthy patterns or behaviors, and that you could realistically hold in place with one another.
  - Ask: "What simple agreements or rules would prevent those things from happening?" Alternatively, you could ask, What do you want to be able to count on from everyone else on this team? Or what rule do you want to be able to count on every teammate following? Example: Check in with the team before making a decision that affects everyone.
  - You'll likely come up with many agreements, so consolidate them down to five or fewer so there aren't too many to remember or follow.

- **Watch for vagueness.** Phrases like "Respect others" are great as team values, but they get dicey as agreements or rules, because everyone can interpret them differently. Discuss what might activate the value as a team rule or agreement until you get to something specific and behavioral that's testable.

- **Set each other up to succeed.** If you're silently expecting people to decide, show up, or react a particular way, yet it's consistently unclear or not happening, create an agreement about it!

- **Agree to hold one another accountable.** For agreements to work, everyone has to be in on creating them and agree to hold them. Commit to one another, including committing to calling it and being called on it when agreements are broken.

- **Post team agreements in your shared space.** Reference them, give them focus, follow them, and call them.

- **Check in with your team about the agreements.** How are we doing on each one (maybe on a scale of 1 to 5)? What do we need to adjust?

- **Check out Blair Singer's book** *Team Code of Honor,* for the "Source of Mastery" process.

"Open collaboration encourages greater accountability, which in turn fosters trust."

–Ron Garan

3.

CALL IT, OWN IT, MOVE ON

HOW TO CALL THINGS OUT EASILY WITHOUT DRAMA

When your team needs this:

- When a team rule has been broken
- When an agreement isn't kept
- When a conflict has happened
- When a ball has been dropped

Why your team needs this:

Most of us don't have great models of how to hold each other accountable in a way that's easy, drama-free, and quick. We spend way too much time weighing how or whether or not to say something or to let go of being upset after we've been called out because we don't have the better tools. Now you will.

When someone breaks an agreement, call it. If a teammate can't see it to call themselves out, it's up to a teammate to call it from a place of commitment to the team. Then own it, clean it up, and reset with the team. If agreements are getting broken consistently, check in with the team to see if it's an unrealistic agreement or if something else needs to shift in order to keep it. Be sure to say what you'd like to have happen (what, how, when), find out what the other person would like to have happen, then get agreement on a plan. Then you can count on it.

UNDERSTAND:

It's easy to say "I'm straightforward and call things out," but it's a different thing to do it consistently, in a way that people can hear, adjust, and move productively and quickly through with it, without drama. You want people to own their actions and choices, not get defensive, and then move forward with some accountability, right? Even if they intellectually know that having that conversation is the right thing to do, it's still tricky to do and they may not know where to start. People have different ways of communicating (ranging from aggressively confrontational to avoidant and vague), which often get in the way of the message or outcome itself.

Having an agreed-upon approach to calling things out makes it simple, straightforward, and actionable.

START:

- Adopt this ➧ mantra. The message: We're not dwelling on it but calling it, doing what's needed to own it (to repair trust, etc.), and moving forward, on to the next things! This keeps the process of

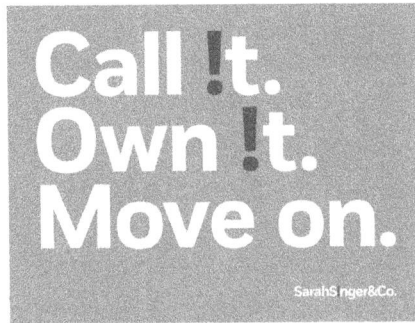

Call !t.
Own !t.
Move on.

SarahSinger&Co.

talking about what's *not* working moving right along without dragging it out. It's like ripping off a Band-Aid.

- As the leader, model calling *yourself* out. You might be used to the role of calling others out, yet for your team to take the risk of calling *themselves* out, they need to see you do it in full accountability via a little vulnerability (sharing that you're not perfect), making it safe for them to be honest.

- If someone breaks an agreement, call it. Ideally, the person will call themselves out; if not, someone else should call it. When calling out other things, the simple OTFD Model below will keep the other person listening and help you say everything you need to say directly and easily in a way that moves things forward. Credit to my friends at Quantum Learning Network, who've been teaching this simple tool for decades in their programs the world over.

The OTFD Model (remember it as Open The Front Door):

- **O = Observation.** State what behaviorally occurred, without judgment attached, in a "fly-on-the-wall" style. This gets you and the other person to the same moment in time of the occurrence. *"When we met last week, we agreed that we'd each have our parts done by this morning so the next phase could start immediately. The piece you're working on isn't complete yet, and we can't start the next phase until it is."*

- **T = Thought.** State your thought, opinion, concern, or assessment about what happened. *"The team's ready to go with the next phase, and the timeline's tight. We need your piece to move forward. I'm concerned about now needing to rush the next phase to hit our overall deadline."*

- **F = Feeling.** State your feeling about the situation. *"I'm frustrated."*

- **D = Desire.** State what you'd like to have happen. This will sound like a request, which gives the other person an opportunity to move forward with a solution. *"Can we get your piece in here and then reassess our plan so we don't short-change the deliverable?"*

"Decency is avoiding disrespect, not avoiding disagreement. Integrity is trying to get it right, not being right."

–Adam Grant

4.

CONFRONT OR AVOID?

HOW TO SEE AND ADAPT YOUR CONFLICT STYLE WITHIN THE TEAM

When you need this:

Every day as you communicate

Why you need this:

Friction, conflict, and upset are normal on teams, and that's true more so for teams working with high stakes. A critical determiner of healthy vs. dysfunctional dynamics on teams isn't the presence of those conflicts but the pattern of what people *do* when those upsets happen. The pattern of how you tend to respond (as a leader and teammate) defines you to others more than you realize, and it impacts your team daily.

UNDERSTAND:

- Every day, people irritate, frustrate, and disappoint one another, usually unintentionally. Sometimes they do it in big ways, sometimes in little ways, and sometimes in small ways that are repeated every day, which then make them *feel* big, like a pebble in your shoe that you've walked on all day.

- We have a spectrum of choices regarding how we handle an upset, ranging from complete avoidance to aggressive confrontation. Where we land on that spectrum directs the dynamic of the team

- While there's a spectrum of choices and conflict styles, the two extremes of Confronter and Avoider are surprisingly common.

AVOIDER

- **Avoiders** don't like confrontation and will tolerate or reroute a *lot* to avoid it. For them to call something out directly, it has to be *really* bad. Their internal dialogue is driven by their discomfort with confronting, so they justify avoidance as not worth the drama, not really that big of a deal, or something that will resolve itself.

- Persistent or recurring upsets get swallowed, internalized, or normalized, and act as an extra weight of negative energy (repressed, unaddressed upsets).

Extreme costs of the Avoider, happening right now:

- Brilliant individuals will quit a team rather than confront someone or something.

- Avoidant teams splinter rather than attempt to address conflicts directly, because it seems too daunting or like too much for them to take on.

- Possibly talented people stagnate because avoidant bosses won't push them, or they dissolve into bitter invisibility when kept in a position for too long — their avoidant boss would rather work around them for years than disrupt the status quo and push them to improve.

- Teams settle for mediocre status or performance rather than calling out what to stop, start, or push to get better.
- Repressed upsets lead to resentment, then passive-aggressive behavior, then "shallowing," in which people pull back, play small, stop trusting, and become guarded, with the team getting just a fraction of them.

CONFRONTER

- **Confronters** love directness, like to call things out, and see confrontation as truthfulness. The sooner they call things out, the better, they believe.
- They have a hard time trusting when they see Avoider patterns ("How can I trust you if I know you're likely holding something back?").
- They believe "no news is good news." They expect that if someone has an upset with them, they'll speak up about it.

Extreme costs of the Confronter, happening right now:

- When it turns accusatory, combative, or hostile, psychological safety is ruined. (See Chapter 1 for more on psychological safety.)
- When someone is confrontational from a place of unchecked anger, frustration, or aggression, it threatens the team's psychological safety.
- Extreme confronters can cause lasting trauma or create unintentionally hostile team cultures because they push too far, too often.

The Everyday Dynamic

To the confronter, if there's something to call out, they'll call it (the sooner, the better for them).

To the avoider, something has to be *really* bad for them to call it out. So, every time the confronter calls something out, the avoider thinks it must be *really* bad, even though it might not be. Every time the avoider doesn't call something out, the confronter thinks everything must be great, even though it might not be. This functions as a vicious daily cycle of misunderstanding.

START:

- **If you're an avoider**, push yourself to be more direct. People can't know your expectations and change or address what you need them to unless you tell them.

- **If you're a confronter**, watch your tone and check in. Structure what you say in a way that people can hear you without feeling attacked. Otherwise, they'll miss your point and you'll just drive avoiders further into avoidance.

- **Aim for intentional directness.** Here, you're not avoiding and not confrontational — you're being kind and clear.

- **Use the OTFD Model** as a way to address issues.

- **Do a weekly check in** to facilitate a team's efficient, direct process. Once people have shared language and structure around it, speaking directly to issues is less daunting, and you can help one another do it. (More on this in the next chapter!)

- **Call it. Own it. Move on!** Adopt this mantra as a team approach. Avoiders love the quickness and the focus on moving on. Confronters love the directness. Make this an agreement on your team, and put it on the wall. Then, practice it! (You'll find examples in Chapter 3.) Once everyone agrees to it, there's both permission and expectation for avoiders to get more direct, which gets things moving.

"It turns out that trust is in fact earned in the smallest of moments. It is earned not through heroic deeds, or even highly visible actions but through paying attention, listening, and gestures of genuine care and connection."

–Brene Brown

5.

CHECKING IN
HOW TO KEEP THE MOST IMPORTANT COMMUNICATION FLOWING

When and where you need this:

- Weekly
- After a team event (competition, presentation, phase of the project)
- When there's something "up" with the team

Why you need this:

You and your teammates are moving quickly, sometimes in rhythm, sometimes not. It's easy to assume alignment when there isn't any, to get frustrated about small things, and to swallow issues instead of working through them directly. These kinds of situations can accumulate quickly, and they slow the team down.

The most common challenge area in teams is communication — the lack of it, inefficiency of it, misunderstanding of it, or withholding of it. True teams check in early and often, with a structured, focused approach that cuts right to what needs to be said. This keeps issues cleared out, alignment on track, learnings feeding your productivity, drama at bay, and that elusive "team chemistry" actually happening.

UNDERSTAND:

- Research now validates that, if trust, openness of communication, and sync aren't there, people hold back, consciously and unconsciously. This is the core of psychological safety, which is the single biggest difference between teams that thrive and teams that don't. (See Chapter 1 for more details.)

- Giving structure to team communication makes things that are otherwise hard to talk about easy!

- Great teams check in with one another as a daily practice to keep little issues from becoming big obstacles to their fast progress, and they call timeouts when the pressure is most intense so they can pivot as needed and keep thoughts, approach, and energy aligned.

- Talking with your team all the time is different than checking in.

- You already know from experience that you can talk with someone every single day without ever broaching the one thing that really needs to be addressed and could shift everything (let alone all the small things that could be tightened up, tweaked, or improved), right?

For efficiency and flow, you need a simple, intentionally structured, check-in process that's designed to quickly get straight to what needs to be surfaced for everyone to gather speed to move forward with clarity and progress. I've got options for you...

START:

Adopt and introduce the mantra of my favorite six words (**Call it. Own it. Move On!)** during regular check-ins. It keeps the somewhat uncomfortable process of talking about what's *not* working moving without dragging it out.

The more you do these check-ins as a consistent practice, the more people will come ready to share and listen to how the team can get better.

THE DAILY HUDDLE STAND-UP

Why: It gets a team quickly into each other's world and on the same page for the day, providing a quick visual + verbal + physical kickstart of connectedness. This creates mental and emotional resonance for the rest of the day.

When: First thing in the morning at a set time every day. Typical length: five to ten minutes.

How: Huddle the team. Once the time's been set, people in other meetings will know that the daily huddle will interrupt for just ten minutes at XX:00 because it's *that* important.

Have a standing, engaging agenda, and rotate who leads it each day. Here's a sample agenda:

1. **Burning Issues:** Anything people need to "get up and out" for the team to know. For example, *Today's my birthday!"*

2. **Move**: A quick physical stretch or movement to mentally, emotionally, and physically wake up together. Try BrainGym or Improv.

3. **Wins:** Progress made in the past twenty-four hours. For instance, "*Our sales are up five percent today!"*

4. **What/when/where.** These are the logistics lineup for the day. Examples include *"Project X is meeting with stakeholders in the space today"* and *"Whitney is working remotely today, yet available."*

5. **One-word whip.** Each person quickly picks and says their one word for the day. This helps focus them, fire them up, etc.

THE THREE-PART CORE CHECK-IN

Why: The check-in creates space and a process for the "unspoken" to get up and out (*"So glad we got that called out!"*), for progress to be seen (*"Wow! Look at how far we've come!"*), and for smart iteration to occur (*"Awesome idea — this will make a difference right away!"*).

When: Ideally, this should be done weekly, but you can do it daily if needed. The more you do this, the faster it gets. This can be ten minutes or two hours, depending on how deep you want to go and how many unspokens are backlogged in the team.

How: Get the team together and make three columns (+, − , Δ).

Get people sharing their thoughts by asking the following three questions about the team process:

+ **What's working?**

− **What's not working?**

Δ **What do we want to change?** (in our dynamics, process, etc.)

Note: There are no wrong answers. The *faster* people can get their thoughts up and out, the better. Encourage building on one another's ideas. As the facilitator, listen in order to develop a sense of when people need to discuss the points or just move quickly to action.

VARIATION: THE TIMEOUT CHECK-IN

When: As in a basketball game, use timeouts, in the midst of an otherwise go-time (a competition, intense practice or work session, presentation, etc.), when you need to pause everything, interrupt a direction, then quickly reset and realign.

The postmortem debrief *after* something's done is important, yet it's too late to get real-time learning or make key pivots. So, using the three-point check in *midway* through a process enables the team to pivot while it still counts!

How: Call a timeout, huddle the team (stay standing to keep it moving), and empower everyone to be able to call one in the midst of the fray or pressure, bringing the team together to reset quickly. Once you're huddled, call out pluses, minuses, and deltas.

Call it. Adjust It. Move on!

At the end, you want to shout out "Awesome!" then put hands in the middle, and GO!

VARIATION: THE TACTICAL DEBRIEF CHECK-IN

When: After a key action, like a meeting, a project, a game, a performance, a push, etc., huddle the team and then use your Three-Part Check-in frame for a tactical debrief.

+	**–**	**△**
What worked?	**What didn't work?**	**What do we want to change out of this?**

High-stakes, quick-learning teams *never* skip this part. Navy Seal teams call this the "AAR" (After-Action Response), and they hold it as one of the most important, non-negotiable practices of their culture of psychological safety, agile learning, and preparedness for anything. The sooner it's done, the better! As a leader, make sure you're calling out your *own* minuses right away. This instantly opens it up for your team to call out and own theirs, too.

At the end, you want to shout out "Awesome!" then put hands in the middle, and GO!

THE EPISODE PROCESSING CHECK-IN

Why: Stuff happens, and people feel the impact. Individuals and teams don't always have a clean path to process what happened in a way that acknowledges it and moves them forward constructively and quickly. Having a simple model to facilitate through it easily is gold and can make the difference between a healthy team and a dysfunctional team.

When: The team has just experienced something big (a major change, pressure, win, loss, etc.), and you need to make it count for something by facilitating constructive meaning out of it for everyone.

How: Get everyone in the room, and ask the following four questions:

1. **Facts:** What actually happened? Were there surprises? Key moments? Keep to the facts of what, when, and where. Watch out for opinions posing as facts, such as "Then X did the worst thing".

2. **Feelings:** What feelings came up for you? For others? What were the highs and lows? Watch here for judgments posing

as feelings. Anything that starts with "I felt that..." is a judgment, not a feeling.

3. **Findings:** What can you/we learn? Ask how and why. Why did it have this kind of impact? Did it work or not work? How did we get here? Where else do you see this pattern happening? What are you realizing now, after the fact?

4. **Future:** What do you/we want to take away from this? What's the learning for us here? What do we want to take action on or do differently because of this?

"Fail fast" only works if a fail is processed into a learning, which most teams don't know how to do quickly or thoroughly. "Celebrate wins" is usually just high-fives or a happy hour, which misses the process to transfer the win into more future wins. The episode processing check-in gives you a guide to both. With it, your team will start actively, vocally learning through experiences together and making faster progress.

THE ONE-WORD WHIP QUICK CHECK

When: Do this during the last closing minute of a session, process, meeting, or competition.

Why: This helps give the team closure, gives every person a chance to be heard, and facilitates and instant processing of their experience and "meaning making."

How: Get everyone together (in a circle is best, so everyone can see everyone else and they're not just talking to you at the front). Ask everyone to quickly...

"Think of one word to capture this session for you."

(You could also say: "one word to capture what you're taking away from this," "one word to capture what you got out of this," or "one word to capture what this means for you.")

Once the first person shares their word, "whip" around the circle, with each person saying their word.

This exercise is powerful because everyone gets a turn and it's only one word, so it pushes everyone to rapidly reflect on their experience, check in with themselves, and synthesize it into a word. They walk away continuing the reflection you began for them, which is exactly the ripples you want to start. This check-in is always gratifying for everyone in the circle, often profound, and always a moment of connection for the group.

Healthy, kick-ass teams check in early and often, with process tools like these. These check-ins keep issues cleared out, alignment on track, drama at bay, learnings feeding productivity, and that elusive "team chemistry" actually happening. You can do this, too. You can call timeouts when the pressure is highest to ensure team momentum, alignment of thought, and approach. You can do it in regular check-ins to keeps little issues from becoming obstacles to fast progress, surface essential insights, and pivot to improve the work as you go. This practice will facilitate forward motion for your team and cement learning, clearing out those little things that would otherwise waste the team's energy as they ruminated and internalized in the background of their thinking.

"The quality of your life is in direct proportion to the amount of uncertainty you can comfortably live with."

—Tony Robbins

6.

STEP OUT

HOW TO GET EVERYONE OUT OF THE COMFORT ZONE AND BE OKAY WITH IT

When and where you need this:

- At the beginning of a new project or challenge
- When the team is getting pushed
- Before a big step, at game time, during a risky action, or the first time something new is introduced
- When someone is doubting their next step

Why you need this:

If you're taking on a new frontier vs. sticking with the status quo, then you've theoretically already stepped out of your comfort zone. It means you're committing to playing bigger, which will pay rewards back in growth, challenges, satisfaction, and pride. Meanwhile, that little voice in your head is messing with you. At the moments you predict *and* the many you won't, it pipes up to try to convince you to take the safer, more reliable path. This happens to every innovative star and team and is part of the breaking-norms process. It can either fuel your team or stop you dead in your tracks. Let's go for the fuel option...

UNDERSTAND:

- Comfort Zone (CZ) is what's known, practiced, tested, routinized, trusted, leaned on, and expected. Each person on your team has their own CZ, and the team has a CZ, too.

- Breakthrough performance and innovation by definition occurs *outside* of the comfort zone in thoughts, processes, choices, orientation, measurement of "results," and even the rhythm of your day.

- Growth happens on the edges of the CZ, as we push, step, or leap out from a place of strength.

- We each have a little voice in our head. Sometimes it's our biggest cheerleader, sometimes our biggest critic.

- Leaving the CZ threatens your little voice, which wants to keep you safe, expert, and looking good. It might pipe up.

- Stepping out of the CZ is exciting and important, yet it can feel like the "danger zone."

- Outside the CZ is the "Learning Zone" (LZ). Learning is messy, and looks and feels the opposite of being an expert, yet it also defines growth.

- If we go *too* far out of our CZ, our learning stops, as our brain goes into fight/flight/freeze mode.

- Stepping out is taking a risk, not knowing how it will go. That puts you into a place of vulnerability, a necessary prerequisite to courage, which is now required.

- The first few times you step out, it often goes poorly. When that occurs, you might feel the impulse to jump back into the CZ and do something safer, more reliable. Debrief +, −, Δ, then step back out and put it to use. That's learning, defined.

- The feedback we get when we fail often determines what comes next. When people can step out, fail, and take risks, knowing that their leader and team will support and acknowledge them (vs. punish, humiliate, or pay retribution), they learn faster. When they can't, they hold back.

- The more your team can comfortably and safely step out of the CZ into the LZ, the faster it will grow, then accelerate its growth.

- Within your field, you're surrounded by people who deliberately do *not* step out to innovate. As you choose to step out, the difference between you and them might sharpen. They might act as your little voice might, so watch out for that.

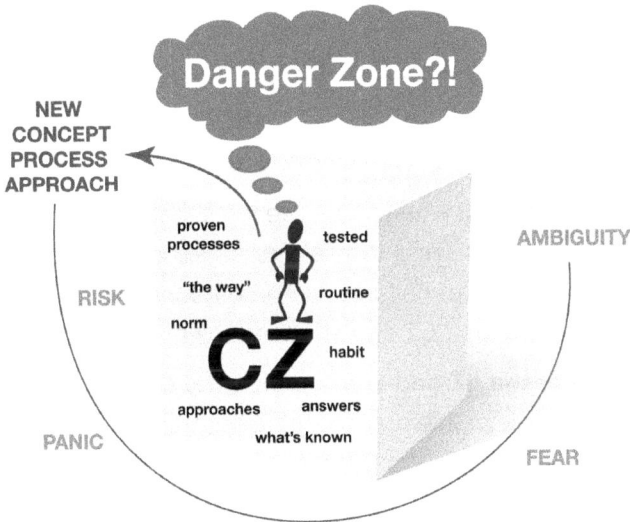

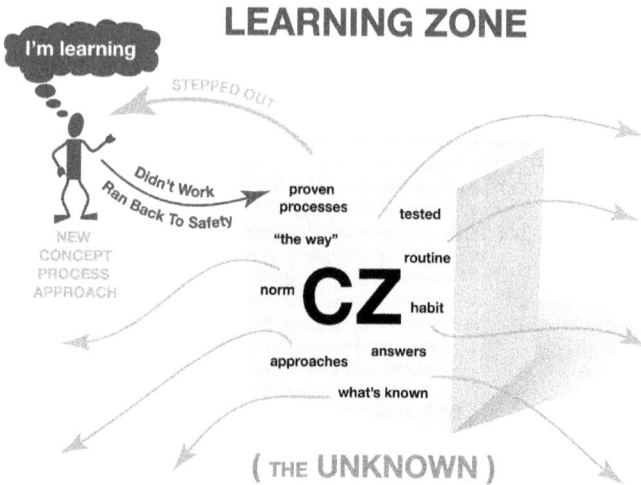

LEARNING ZONE

I'm learning

STEPPED OUT

Didn't Work
Ran Back To Safety

NEW CONCEPT PROCESS APPROACH

proven processes

tested

"the way"

routine

norm **CZ** habit

answers

approaches

what's known

(THE **UNKNOWN**)

START:

- **Check in about the CZ vs. the LZ** for your team and also as individuals.

  - Where are we in our CZ? Where are we out of it?

- **Agree to call out** when someone feels that they, a teammate, or the team is playing too safe or small, instead of stepping out. Also agree to call out when someone feels like they're too far out of their CZ and shutting down.

- **Celebrate the LZ and step outside the CZ as a team!** Do it daily or weekly. Give positive reinforcement to any steps your team takes outside the CZ.

- **Help one another be learners.** Do things as a team that are out of your CZ and put you in learning mode together (vs. prove-it mode or expert mode). Do regular "learning moment" share-outs.

- **Find your CZ busters.** What gets you to step out when you're stuck or panicking? Let your team know. Have the whole team think about it and share their ideas, then help one another step out with any of these ideas:

- Encouragement and reassurance from others to go for it
- A cause to rally for
- A partner to do it with them
- A direct challenge — something or someone to prove wrong
- Someone else to go first
- Scrutinizing the pros and cons in a personal cost-benefit analysis
- Desperation (can't take it anymore)
- Inspiration

Create the space and the process for your team to learn fast, and support one another in it. With that, they'll push boundaries, further accelerating their learning!

"Tell me and
I forget,
teach me and
I may remember,
involve me and
I learn."

—Benjamin Franklin

7.

GET IT

HOW TO MAKE LEARNING EASIER & KEEP PUSHING UNTIL IT'S SOLID

When and where you need this:

- At the beginning of a new project or challenge as a team
- When you feel like you should be moving or "getting it" faster than you are
- When you're feeling like you used to be competent but are now out of your element
- When it's feeling more challenging than gratifying

Why you need this:

In the world of pushing what's possible, things likely feel different than when you were in a comfortable role of ease, expertise, and competence. You're here on a team that's seeking another level, because the talent and expertise you demonstrated elsewhere earned you a spot to forge a new path forward. Nice! Except you might be feeling unsettled, not like an expert so much anymore (but craving that feeling), out here in the learning zone of innovation. Right?

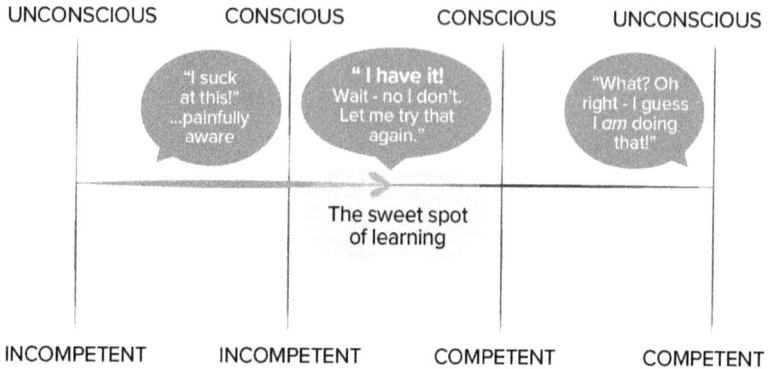

UNDERSTAND:

- For anything you do, you're at a certain level of *competence* (how well can you do it), with a certain amount of *consciousness* about that competence (how much you're thinking about it as you do it).

- *Unconscious-Incompetent (UI):* not knowing that you don't know. You don't know and you don't even realize it. *Example*: anything you've never heard of, for which you're also incompetent.

- *Conscious-Incompetent (ICI):* realizing that you don't know something or can't do it. *Example*: When you first try something out of your CZ, you're painfully aware of how bad you are at it.

- *Conscious-Competent (CC):* being able to do it, with conscious intentionality. *Example*: doing something well, thinking through it.

- *Unconscious-Competent (UC):* able to do it without thinking about it, either from natural talent or by practicing to the point of expertise. *Example*: anything you excel in to the point of not needing to think about it.

- We get important fulfillment of and an increase in our self-esteem in doing what we do best (UC mode).

- We get rewarded for competence. We associate CC and UC as good, UI and CI as bad.

- In the innovation and breakthrough space, the opposite is true: The more you can be a learner, the better, as you explore, iterate, create, test, push, and accomplish (UC= stagnation)!

- That sweet spot of learning between CI and CC is clutch; it's where people either get destroyed or get tough.

- In the growth process, you're deliberately stepping out of the comfort of UC into learner mode. As you learn, you'll spend a lot of time feeling incompetent, which is unsettling. As soon as you add something to your UC bucket, you move back into learner mode CC for the next piece. While it's a progressive process, it's not linear. You'll bounce around on the spectrum.

START:

- Make space for every person on the team to be a learner, and set an expectation that everyone has something they're pushing themselves on in learner mode.

- Visually track your learnings as a team and as individuals all the time (on the UI-UC spectrum). This will show you how you're making progress and satisfy that need for competence.

- Make sure the team (and each team member) spends significant time in UC strength mode to balance learning mode.

- Identify places, roles, and parts of the process where you can use your natural talent and strengths. Make sure you're using them every day.
- Support one another as learners. Pay attention to teammates' level of stress, and make sure everyone's getting a balance of playing from their strengths and stretching their learning.

"Life is not
a problem
to be solved
but a reality
to be
experienced."

–Soren Kierkegaard

8.

GET "REALITY"

HOW TO REFRAME ANYTHING THAT HAPPENS TO KEEP THE OUTLOOK HEALTHY

When and where you need this:

- In moments of frustration, tension, or disappointment
- When you or the team is stuck on something that happened
- When you notice yourself or the team getting quiet, holding back
- When you're judging someone, or interpreting something that's happened negatively

Why you need this:

You trust your gut and make quick decisions and judgment calls based on your assessment of things, both out loud and in your head. So does everyone else on your team. That can be awesome — or really off, because the "reality" you're basing your decisions on may not always be as solid as you think it is. Our ability to interpret what we experience and see into meaning is both our gift and our challenge. What happens, and what we then make it mean, are not at all the same, yet we collapse them together. In negative moments, that can derail everything, yet you can re-steer it.

UNDERSTAND:

- Things happen all around us, and we interpret them as reality. This can go many different ways, and it happens hundreds of times per day for every one of us.
    - Example: *What happened:* You're about to cross a street and see a bus coming. *Meaning you made:* Crossing right now is a bad idea.
- Circle #1 (in the illustration on page 61) is objective.
- Circle #2 is subjective — it's just an interpretation (or story) we create.
- We collapse #1 and #2 together and call it "reality," often without question. *Example*: I almost got killed by a bus.
- Sometimes the meaning we make causes upset, stress, angst, and frustration, and we can get stuck there unproductively, unconsciously.
- Circle #2 is where upsets start and grow, yet it's also where we ironically have the most control.
- We make meaning through our personal filters. Under pressure or outside our CZ, Circle #2 might be colored by our own self-doubt or fear. For example, "That presentation was awful. Maybe I'm not the right person to do this."
- Our filters of meaning making can be colored by certain people (see Chapter 10 for more details).

Circle #1   Circle #2

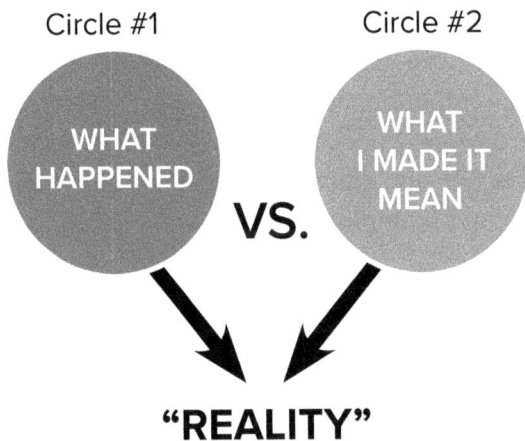

"REALITY"

START:

- Notice your patterns of meaning making, and talk about it with your team. When do you go negative in that second circle? Who on the team stays positive when the others go negative? What are the triggers for you as individuals and as a team to go negative?

- Bust out these circles when someone on the team is upset or when you're going negative as a team.

- Draw them and then fill them in with what actually happened ("Bob said X" or "Y decision was made.") and what you're making it mean (list all the things you're saying in your head and out loud — no censoring).

- Next, ask yourselves about the second circle: "Do I know *that* to be true?" (Answer: "No, it's just a story.") Then ask, "Is it helping us/me move forward in a healthy way to see it that way?" (Answer: "No, we're swirling in angst.") Then draw a third circle and force yourselves to come up with a different, more productive meaning than what's in the second circle.

- Call each other out on your meaning making in moments of negativity or frustration, challenging yourself and one another with "Separate your circles," "Is that what happened or what you made it mean?" and "What's another second circle you could make up here that's also plausible, yet healthier for me/us?"

"Every time you are tempted to react in the same old way, ask if you want to be a prisoner of the past or a pioneer of the future."

–Deepak Chopra

9.

UPSETS HAPPEN
HOW TO DISMANTLE ANY AGITATION INTO A SOLVABLE PROBLEM

When and where you need this:

- When you're setting up as a team or in any conversation where one of the purposes is to "get aligned"
- When you notice yourself getting irritated or upset, especially with another person
- When you notice someone else getting irritated or upset, especially with another person

Why you need this:

Irritations, conflicts, and upsets happen between teammates all the time, yet we often don't acknowledge them until they feel big. You and your team need to move nimbly and quickly, and can't have upsets (big or small) clouding the clarity and connection between you or distracting your thinking.

Like that little pebble in your shoe that causes you to limp by the end of the day if it's left alone, upsets slow you down; they get in the way of the collaboration, ideation, and flow you need with your team in order to play full out with one another and create standard-breaking work. You need to be able to call things out quickly and easily, so things don't build up. So, let's get you set up another way.

UNDERSTAND:

- You have expectations of everyone around you all the time, including how people should act, react, and show up in your interactions. So does everyone else.

- Everyone also has upsets all the time, ranging from barely an annoyance to a huge confrontation or standoff of avoidance. This is completely normal.

- We don't have great models or norms for how to communicate effectively in moments of upset.

- Every upset breaks down to an expectation that's been unmet. (Read that bullet again: It's key!)

- You also have expectations of how things *should* go (how people should react, etc.).

- We're not always aware of our own expectations until they're *unmet* (and sometimes not even then).

- We unintentionally stay in the emotion and drama of upsets because it's what's most palpable to us.

- Moving to the expectation that's been unmet shifts our focus from emotional swirl to a problem to solve.

- The more you clarify and articulate your expectations ahead of time, the fewer upsets occur.

- The faster you can identify the unmet expectations under upsets as they occur, the faster you can let go of upsets and get into alignment with others going forward.

START:

- When an upset occurs for an individual or the team, check in to find the expectation underneath it that's been unmet. Then ask yourself if that expectation was:
  - Something you were aware you had before the upset
  - Articulated at any point and understood and acknowledged by the other person
  - Realistic and fair
- Then call it. Have a conversation in which you own the upset, own your expectation, and reset.
- Get in the practice of identifying and voicing those silent expectations with your teammates, partners, and stakeholders early in the process and get to agreement. The more agreement you have going in, the fewer upsets occur.

UPSET

BARELY
a thing

HUGE
confrontation
or standoff

EXPECTATION UNMET

"People will forget
what you said.
People will forget
what you did.
But people will
never forget
how you made
them feel."

—Maya Angelou

10.

IN-10-TION

HOW TO GET JUDGMENT OUT OF THE WAY OF GREATNESS

When you need this:

- As you're beginning to work with someone
- When you're setting up your team in the beginning
- When you notice yourself getting repeatedly annoyed, impatient, or frustrated with someone

Why you need this:

You've likely experienced one of these situations:

a) Someone believed in you, even when you doubted yourself. On a scale of 1 to 10, they had a "10" over your head.

b) Someone doubted or didn't believe in you, even when you knew you were better than their judgment. On that scale of 1 to 10, they had a "1" or "2" over your head. In each of those cases, they didn't even have to say it — you knew by their tonality, their approach, and the way they gave you feedback on what they thought about you. How did it affect you?

Maybe you've experienced both situations. I know you've been (and maybe still are) on the other side of each, too, either believing in someone or being their biggest fault-finder, even

69

if it was only in your head. Even when they aren't expressed, those judgments actually have more power over us than we think, especially if the person holding those numbers holds rank/authority/influence in relation to us.

In looking at what ultimately determines a person's level of performance or mastery, all the skill, motivation, and experience they bring to it might only be equal to what that influencer thought they could do! Yes, a teammate, boss, or coach's belief or opinion of our capability can determine up to *half* of what we actually produce!

In real time, you and your team need to be able to move and pivot quickly, trusting that others will be with you when you step out. You need to bring game-changing ideas, and hear and some tough feedback sometimes. To do these things as efficiently as possible, you and your teammates need to make sure nothing gets in the way of doing that cleanly, especially something that has that much power. Those numbers over people's heads are already a factor right *now* in how others are able to step into their own potential or not. Those numbers become filters through which we see, hear, and consider everything about/from someone.

This is IN-10-TION. It has more power than you realize, and it can make or break your team's success.

UNDERSTAND:

- We all judge others consciously and subconsciously. It's human nature.

- The numbers you have over other people's heads are more transparent than you think. Just like you *know* when someone has a "2" or a "10" over your head, your team knows the numbers you have over their heads and are affected by them.

- Having a "10" over someone's head means being committed to their growth and believing in their talent and potential. It means being committed to someone's success beyond what they show in the moment and maybe beyond what they believe is possible in themselves. It means having **IN-10-TION** for them.

- Having a "3" over someone's head means not believing in them, their, ability, or their potential or growth. This comes from unresolved upsets or unmet expectations, adopting other people's judgments, or seeing people through negative filters.

- Hearing hard feedback from someone who has a "10" over your head is easier; you know their intent is to make you or the work better and that they believe in you. You're open to their challenge.

- Getting hard feedback from someone who has a "2" over your head is brutal; it feels defeating and personal, as you know they don't believe in you.

- People often perform to the level of other people's judgments. According to Renate Nummela Caine and Geoffrey Caine in their the book, *Education on the Edge of Possibility*, the number you hold over another's head can determine up to *half* of all that contributes to their performance.

START:

- Own the numbers you have over other people's heads. Where the number is low, challenge yourself to address it, find the source, clear old upsets (use OTFD), and find the "10" in them.

- If someone's performance or behavior is a "3," that doesn't mean you have to see *them* as a "3." Separate the behavior from the person, then coach to the gap. Your commitment to their "10" is your grounding to be able to coach them harder, as it's coming from your ruthless commitment to their success. ("Because I believe it's in you.")

Talk about IN-10-TION on your team, and agree to come from a place of pure IN-10-TION, holding "10's" over people's heads. Agree to call it out if you question someone's IN-10-TION, then clear it and reset.

"You can't be that kid standing at the top of the waterslide, overthinking it. You have to go down the chute."

–Tina Fey

11.

SPARK MOTIVATION

HOW TO GET OUT OF YOUR WORLD AND MAKE IT MATTER IN THEIRS (OWNING IT)

When you need this:

- When you're getting yourself motivated or re-motivated
- When you're trying to get someone else engaged or excited
- When you're giving someone a directive

Why you need this:

Our motivation is precious, because it's completely personal and the key to everything else—it's literally the reason we do what we do. When it's there, everything switches on and we accelerate; when it's not, everything is slower and harder.

Think about something on your plate right now that you're motivated about vs. something that you're not. That difference is night and day, right? This determines how you engage, and it translates to outcomes, results, and impact.

Your team is a collection of individuals whose motivation is pivotal in determining what you accomplish together. When you tap into that, you get all of what they each can bring, and your possibility is stacked. When you don't, it's a frustrating crapshoot.

UNDERSTAND:

- Motivators have been thought of as either extrinsic (reward, acknowledgment, or threat from the outside) or intrinsic (satisfaction, interest, or drive from inside of us). While extrinsic is more commonly seen (reward systems, incentives, grades, or carrot + stick), its effect fades fast — it's short-lived and actually kills performance and motivation over time. According to research cited in *Harvard Business Review*, intrinsic motivators are more effective, meaningful, and longer-lasting. They increase performance immediately and over time, and are what high performers need as fuel.

- Our internal little voice asks a universal question when it's assessing if or how to fully engage, listen, or buy in to something we're not already motivated by: WIIFM, or "What's In It For Me?"

- WIIFM is the reason, from one's own perspective, to engage. If something doesn't link to your motivation or isn't something that matters to you, you won't really care about it. Yet if you *do* care, your attention, motivation, and thinking are immediately awakened and engaged.

- Basic WIIFM kicks in whenever someone engages with us at some level. If someone gives us a "why" right from the beginning, everything goes faster.

- There are three deeper human drives that all people share. In our work and performance, when these are satisfied, we're motivated. If they're not, we're not. Your team and teammates need all three of these switched on to be effective. Remember these three drives by this acronym: MAP, which was developed by author Daniel Pink and outlined in his book, *Drive*.

- **Mastery** = our need to feel competent, yet also our need to feel as if we're making progress. So even if you're completely in the Learning Zone (not competent yet), it's still okay if you see that you're making progress, according to the *Harvard Business Review* research noted above.

- **Autonomy** = our sense of choice and agency, moment to moment. Nobody ever did something inspired because they were *told* to — they did it because they *chose* to. Challenge the team and your teammates as a call to action, not as a directive, and you'll see night and day results in motivation.

- **Purpose** = feeling that we and what we *do* matters as part of something bigger than ourselves. When you can see how your piece fits into a greater good, a collective win, or an important cause or mission, your purpose switches on.

- Most of us came from an educational culture of extrinsic motivators, even though it's been shown that they kill creativity and performance over time. You may feel a contrast here and need to reorient. It's worth it.

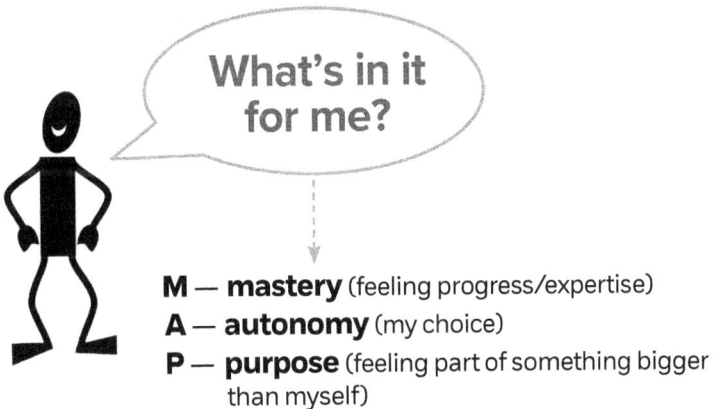

What's in it for me?

M — **mastery** (feeling progress/expertise)
A — **autonomy** (my choice)
P — **purpose** (feeling part of something bigger than myself)

START:

- **Tap WIIFM.** As you approach someone, start with the "why" they'll authentically care most about. You'll save time, and they'll engage immediately.

- **Check in** with yourself and your team on each part of MAP and determine how they're switching on or off. If any of them are off, adjust. Get clear about what switches them on for your teammates and for the collective team.

- **Mastery.** Visually track your learnings and progress weekly as individuals and as a team. Post it on a wall as a constant reminder of how you're making progress.

- **Autonomy.** Own, identify, and claim moments and decisions as your choice.

- **Change directives** into questions the other person can answer yes to, thus tapping their sense of choice. "I need you to..." becomes "Here's the need. Are you game?"

- **Purpose.** Identify and talk about how the work impacts the bigger picture and how individual contributions and presence specifically make a difference in the bigger picture, goal, impact, and team.

When presenting an idea, open with the impact (what it will solve, what it will cause) on the bigger picture.

"Responsibility equals accountability equals ownership. And a sense of ownership is the most powerful weapon a team or organization can have."

—Pat Summitt

12.

ABOVE THE LINE

RESPONDING IN A WAY THAT'S OPEN,
FRANK, AND CONSCIENTIOUS

When you need this:

- When you realize you've dropped the ball in some way
- When you're inside your own head, as you react to things
- With your team, every day

Why you need this:

Mistakes, ball drops, poor word choice, and overreactions happen. We all have moments we're not proud of, yet how we handle those moments tells your team volumes about what they can count on from you and determines whether or not they'll trust you. You need your team to trust one another, consistently own it, and support one another to show their ability to respond from a place of learning and growth.

UNDERSTAND:

- As humans, our instinct is to protect ourselves. Sometimes that messes with our choices.

- Dropped balls without accountability (despite their cause) destabilizes trust between people. Shaky trust is a liability that slows and compromises everything else on your team.

- As soon as we realize we've done something (or missed something) we shouldn't have, we go to a particular place in our mind. That place, and every response from it, sends a message about who we are.

- Reacting **above the line** is owning it. This sends a message that you have the ability to respond in a way that's open, frank, and conscientious, and it preserves your personal power (your actions, your choices, and your responses).

- Reacting in any of these ways is **below the line**:
  - *Lay blame* - blaming it on someone or something else outside of your control
  - *Justify* - creating a reason to explain why it's okay
  - *Deny* - not admitting it or pretending it didn't happen
  - *Quit* - resigning yourself as powerless, unable to respond in any other way

- Below-the-line responses are reactive, normal defense mechanisms we all intuitively have. They also create drama and send a message that you're a person who doesn't take accountability. Most of us also have a default response that's below the line (like you might lay blame as a pattern).

- Even if something below the line is true — it might actually be someone else's fault — it smacks of "excuse" to someone else if you go there first.

- Above the line is harder for our ego, yet it's empowering because it's cleaner. It relays the message that you're transparently human and owning it, increasing trust and credibility.

- The more that teams *call it, own it, and move on,* the faster they learn and move forward, the less need people feel to go below the line, and the less drama there is.

START:

- **Call it. Own it. Move on!** Use the OTFD model to call it out for someone else and call it yourself if you know you need to own it.

- **Come from above the line**, even when it's easier not to, such as when it's someone else's fault. It repairs the tear in trust, after which you can debrief why it happened.

- **Call out below-the-line behavior** with one another. Don't make it a "gotcha" callout but a "Hey! Maybe try that again above the line?" callout. The more you do this, the easier it is to come from above the line.

RESPOND–ABILITY

The Line

QUIT
DENY
JUSTIFY
LAY BLAME

"Where the head goes, the body follows. Perception precedes action. Right action follows the right perspective."

–Ryan Holiday

13.

STATE

HOW TO SPARK, SET, AND CHANGE ENERGY ON THE SPOT

When you need this:

- When you need to focus, spark, calm down, or adjust your energy
- When someone else needs to do the same
- When the team's energy drops
- When you know you're vulnerable to being "thrown off" your game

Why you need this:

Your energy is critical. On a team, it's also both sensitive and contagious. You've experienced the shift in having your outlook and energy either sparked or killed by someone else, right?

This matters more than we thought, because it determines the speed and insight of your ideas, the speed of your learning, and the quality of your performance.

The pressure you're under as a team is significant, and the pressure and stress are real. People who consistently bring it every time, even under pressure, despite the challenge, the day, or the issue at hand, have mastery over something you all need. It's called "State."

UNDERSTAND:

- At any given moment, you're in a particular state, such as bored, excited, focused, annoyed, or inspired.
- State is comprised of three parts: mental, emotional, and physical. They're interconnected all the time
  - Think of your reduced ability to ideate when you're feeling emotionally angry or physically too hot or cold. Or consider the physical surge in your body when you feel elatedly happy.
- Focus, attention, learning, and performance are state-dependent. Your state determines your ability to do those things and to what level.
- Change one of those three parts, and the other two are automatically affected. This is a "state change." It can happen in nanoseconds.
- Some states are super-productive, but some are really unproductive.
- State changes occur constantly and happen due to *outside triggers*, like seeing a particular name come up on caller ID, which instantly makes you anxious or annoyed or happy, or by *choice*, as in when you're feeling slow or sleepy as you work, so you get up to stretch, then feel energized and focused.
- Consistently elite performers intentionally set and change their state as needed.

- You can choose your state and change it at any time, with an intentional change to any of the three parts.
- State is highly contagious, especially in teams. Your positive state lifts others up, and your negative state brings their energy down, even when you're not aware of or intending to do either.
- You can help others spot, choose, and change their state.

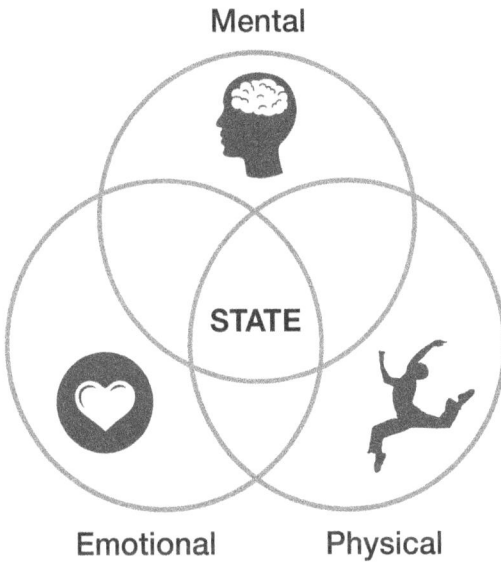

Mental

STATE

Emotional   Physical

START:

- **Spot your state.** Notice the different states you're in throughout the day and what triggers a state change for you, both positively and negatively. This could include people, actions, times, or circumstances.
- **Own your state.** Agree to support one another on the team by owning and managing your own state, keeping it productive

and calling out the need for state changes when attention is waning or performance is falling

- **Check it.** Do state checks with one another before starting together, halfway through what you're doing, and at the end.
- **Set a team state.** Get rituals in place to set a team state before "on" time. These could include one-hand-in huddles, chants, team deep breaths, visualization, etc.
- **Experiment** individually and as a team with state changes by intentionally changing mental, emotional, or physical states in order to shift the overall state.
  - Mental:
    - Visualize a favorite place
    - Read an inspirational quote
    - Visualize yourself crushing the next challenge
  - Emotional:
    - Look at a picture of a favorite person, place or thing
    - Have someone tell you a joke
    - Listen to specific music to calm down, energize, or focus
    - Re-read a great note someone sent you
    - Talk about your passion and your big why
  - Physical:
    - High-five someone
    - Jump
    - Clap
    - Take a quick walk or run
    - Stand instead of sit for a while
    - Brush your teeth or wash your face

"We can change
our lives.
We can do,
have, and be
exactly what
we wish."

—Tony Robbins

14.

BE IT. DO IT. HAVE IT.

HOW TO MAKE TRUE IMPACT EVERY TIME
WHILE EXPANDING YOUR RANGE

When you need this:

- At the beginning of a team, a venture, a project, or before a big presentation, event, competition, etc., as you set course for impact

- As you shift gears from one interaction, event, or time block to another

- After an interaction to understand how you ended up where you did

- When you feel like you keep missing the impact you want to have

Why you need this:

For each member of your team (including you!) to show up as the "best" version of themselves at each moment, you need an accurate, quick tool to pinpoint what that situationally and specifically means, then shift them there moment by moment.

You want your team to be driven by something self-generating, which taps into a drive in them more powerful than just

91

the momentary goal. You want your team to *own* their impact and choices with intention — elevating, accelerating, clarifying, and connecting those choices to make a bigger impact in the moment vs. waiting for you to tell them the next move.

We get in our own way a lot of the time. We say and do one thing, yet our tone, vibe, and impact sends a different message — it might even conflict with what we do and say. You've seen multiple people execute the same steps as another person, yet they get wildly different impacts from those same steps.

This is all related, in the power of three words:

BE.

DO.

HAVE.

It's a helpful frame, yet a quick and powerful impact, behavioral change, and alignment tool.

UNDERSTAND:

We're motivated by purpose — being part of something bigger than ourselves — yet the results we often focus the team on are finite results, not significant enough to tap deep purpose.

The results we're focused on moment to moment have impact farther than we ever plan for or talk about. For any result you're working toward right now, ask yourself, "What impact will that have on me, on the people around me, and on other things?" Whatever your answer, ask yourself the same question again about *that* impact you just determined. What impact will *that* have? Ask this question five layers into the goal, and you'll find the ripple effect you're *already* having. Focus gets to purpose when we get intentional, so what impact do you want to have?

- Every time we say "The end justifies the means," we're saying that the impact we're having in how or what we do isn't good and is costing someone or something else significantly. It matters! So, own the full impact you have, separate from just the metrics you're focused on.

- The steps of your plan, or tweaks to the approach, will expand and get more specific with this more purposeful "have" focus. Ask yourself what you will need to do intentionally differently and how you'll need to do it in order to have that *bigger* impact? This is the "DO."

- We have many versions of ourselves. Some are fantastic, but some are not. Our unconscious default versions — when we're at our normal, our best (are you the inspirer, the cheerleader, or the listener?), *and* when we're at our worst (are you the victim, the steamroller, or the avoider?) — shape everything.

- That version of ourselves that comes through more clearly than we think, even when we're unaware of it. This is the "BE."

- Our self-awareness of our own defaults from moment to moment is very limited, so our self-control of them is thin, especially when triggered by others, even though people sense, trust and respond to who we're BE-ing more than what we say or do. We often come away from an interaction calling out who the other person was BE-ing — "Wow! They were being such a jerk" or "They're such a great partner" — as more impactful than what they did, because it's what we sense and trust to be authentic.

- Who you're BE-ing with your team is affecting them right now.

- How you do what you do completely depends on what version of yourself you're BE-ing in the moment, yet most people never even consider it.

- We have far more options than we think from moment to moment of which version of ourselves we could be. We need a bigger range of motion here.

- Of the many situations and interactions you have in a day, what version you're BE-ing for each one may need to change. For instance, you might really need to go from BE-ing a strategist to a listener to a creator in the first three conversations of the day, but if you didn't intentionally think about it and transition into each of those mindsets before those three meetings, you'd miss the impact you needed to have in them.

START:

- When you're going into projects, meetings, or initiatives, pull the team together and set your course.

- Map it out: Have → Do → Be.

  ○ *What impact do we/I want to **have** in this?* Keep pushing that question to get past just the "result" to talk about the impact of that result, ripple, etc. For every answer you come up with, ask "And then what?" to get to the next ripple layer of bigger impact.

  ○ *What will we/I need to **do** to have that kind of impact?* Focus on what you'll need to do differently than you normally would to realistically have impact beyond what you've already had.

- *Who will we/I need to **be** to do that?* Perhaps brainstorm all the different "hats" you could possibly wear and have that list here as a resource (strategist, partner, listener, risk-taker, advocate, etc.).

- Then, to execute it, step into it the other way. **Be** the version of yourself you intend ➜ **Do** what you need to do ➜ **Have** the impact you intend.

- Once your team gets this frame, use it with one another, asking the questions to get purposeful about approach. It's also a great coaching guide, asking those questions to have someone own their impact, get intentional about what they do to that end, and have more agency, choosing who they're being vs. just unconsciously defaulting or reacting.

- Throughout your days, and when the pressure's on, keep resetting to get intentional.

- Personally, after an occurrence, event, upset, or win, break it down to raise your self-awareness of what happened, the role you played in it, and how you can learn moving forward from it. Use Be/Do/Have as a debrief template:

  - What impact did I *have*?

  - What did I *do* to cause that impact?

  - What version of myself was I *being* to be able to do that?

- Call out your own default BE settings, then intentionally practice new ones, expanding your range.

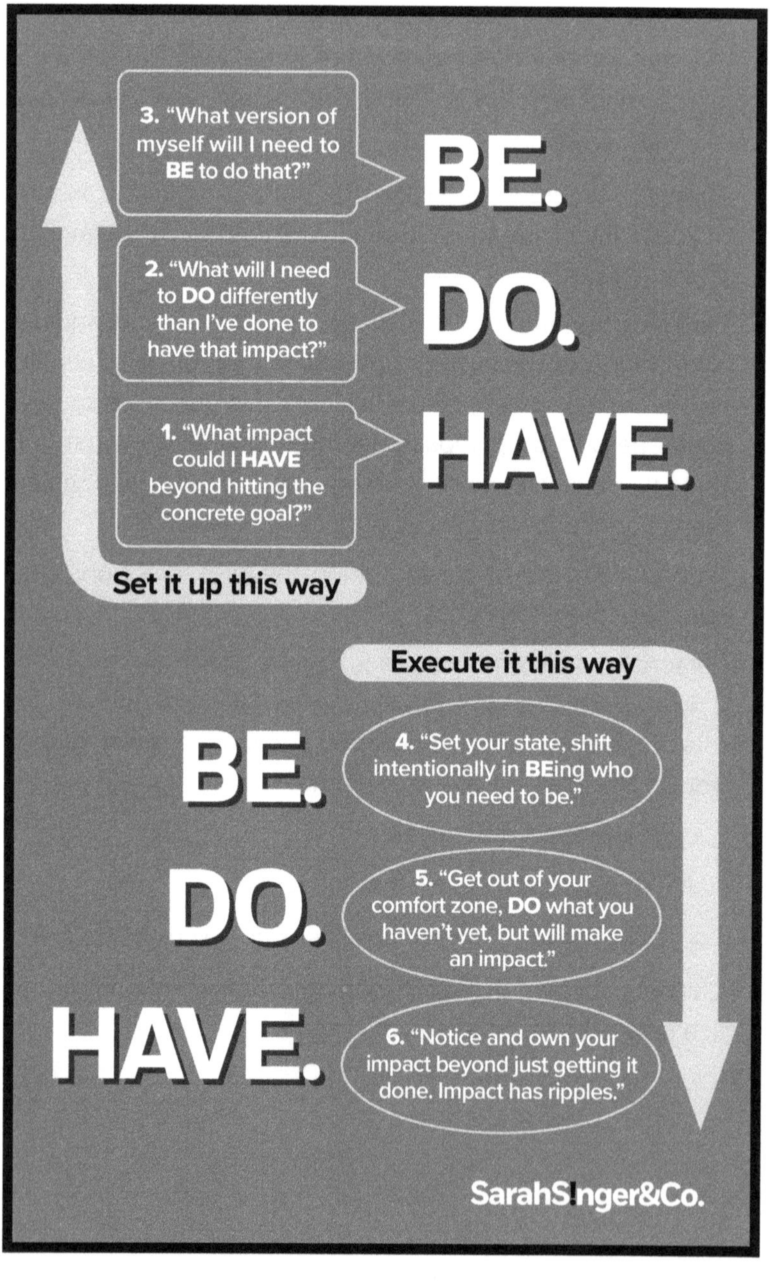
3. "What version of myself will I need to BE to do that?"
BE.
2. "What will I need to DO differently than I've done to have that impact?"
DO.
1. "What impact could I HAVE beyond hitting the concrete goal?"
HAVE.
Set it up this way
Execute it this way
BE.
4. "Set your state, shift intentionally in BEing who you need to be."
DO.
5. "Get out of your comfort zone, DO what you haven't yet, but will make an impact."
HAVE.
6. "Notice and own your impact beyond just getting it done. Impact has ripples."
SarahS!nger&Co.

"Your WHY is not about what you do but about how you do it and the impact you have on others."

–Simon Sinek

15.

GET PERSPECTIVE
LEVERAGING THE PYRAMID OF PERSPECTIVE

When and where you need this:

- When you're revealing the plan for what's going to happen
- When you notice yourself getting stressed by the details
- When you're explaining what needs to be different
- When you feel like you're losing perspective or project focus

Why you need this:

In the swirl of the day to day, it can be easy to lose perspective on the bigger picture and the bigger purpose. What's most immediate is where our attention goes, yet there are many more layers that you need to keep bringing back into focus. You and your team need to be able to get perspective quickly, zooming into the details of the work, then panning back out to see the big picture and purpose, then zooming back in with more insight and drive.

UNDERSTAND:

- Any initiative always includes the layers **Why, What, How, and When** in it. This is called the "pyramid of perspective."

- While some are more obvious than others at times, each layer of the pyramid is important to clearly understand as you and your team create. The key is to keep each layer clear and in proportion to the others, allowing clear perspective.

- We may get sucked into individual layers, which cause us to lose perspective regarding the bigger picture. For example, in the stress of a deadline (When), we can lose sight of the Why we're doing this in the first place, distorting our perspective out of proportion.

- When we skip layers, the process, the team's mindset, and the quality of the work suffers.

  ○ Example: If we're just focusing on How we're doing the work, without the Why we're doing the project in the first place or What we're trying to create, build, or accomplish, we could easily tweak it away from the original purpose

  ○ Another example: If you're just focusing on How someone needs to adjust this or do that differently without first grounding your shared Why and agreed-upon goal (What), it just feels like you're micromanaging them, and there's no buy-in from your teammate.

- When layers are skipped or aren't well-defined, people will fill them in mentally themselves, and often inaccurately (especially the Why).

  ○ Example: I guess you're on my case about changing these little details (How) because you think your ideas are better than mine and just want it your way. (The Why is missing. It could be that the client wanted a change!)

- The higher up the pyramid we go, the more stressed we become.

- The deeper on the pyramid we go toward Why, the broader and more grounded your perspective gets, as we're able to clearly see What, How and When layered proportionally.

- Starting with Why, then adding each layer in order, keeps perspective and the big picture clear. You can go into the details of When and How, yet ground the conversation first with the purpose of Why and What we're creating.

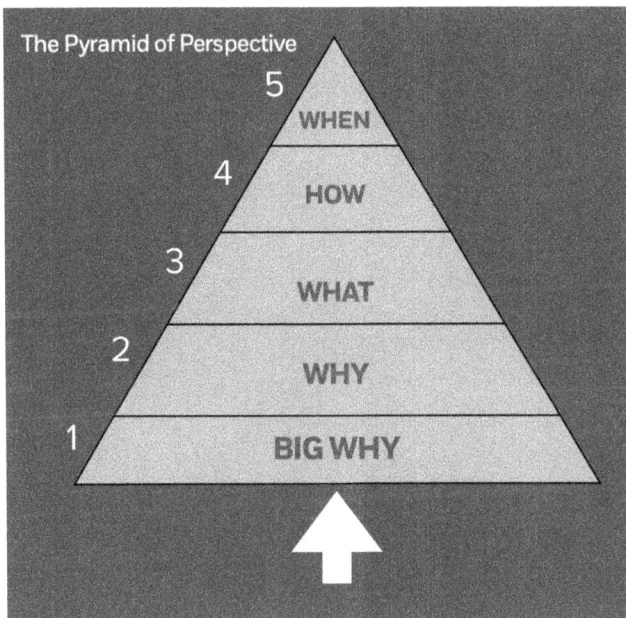

The Pyramid of Perspective

5 — WHEN
4 — HOW
3 — WHAT
2 — WHY
1 — BIG WHY

START:

- Huddle your team to define and get alignment on every layer of the pyramid for your project, starting with the bottom.
- Identify the sublayers of Why (in-the-moment Why, logistical Why, budgetary Why, company Why, need-you're-solving-for Why, or global Why).
- Begin every project, work session, meeting, and request with Why, then add the other layers in order. When you do, people will engage from the beginning, keep the details in relative perspective, and stay grounded.
- When giving feedback, making requests, or asking for changes, start with your "for the purpose of…" Why first, which gives you grounding.
  - Example: "So we can be on the same page in expectations as we work together."

"Pressure is a
privilege –
it only comes
to those
who earn it."

–Billie Jean King

16.

PERTURBATION
MANAGING THE PRESSURE OF TRANSFORMATION

When you need this:

- When you're feeling pressure or stress
- When you're wrestling with a tough situation
- When you're unclear about it being "worth it" to stay in the game

Why you need this:

Pressure is real, especially for you and your team as you perform. It's in the drive to create, show, and demonstrate something new within certain restraints, with stakeholders watching. It's in everyone's expectations as you disrupt the norm to create a shift.

Consider the transformation of a piece of coal into a diamond; pressure created that transformation. It's in nature, organizations, your team's process, and your own, too. While it's uncomfortable to be *in* it, it's necessary in order to truly shift.

UNDERSTAND:

- Pressure creates **perturbation,** as in "to perturb," which is a literal disruption to a status.

- A person, team, process, or organization feels perturbation before a shift happens.

- As pressure rises, things definitely "heat up" — our actual body temperature rises — and we metaphorically sense things "getting hot" as we press on.

- In the chemical perturbation of wood shifting into coal, off-gassing will happen as the shift starts to occur. The carbon releases physical gas, yet in teams, people might opt out or leave ("It's too hot for me — I'm out.").

- After a certain threshold of pressure is reached over time, what's been under pressure and perturbation transforms into a different, stronger, more stable structure, able to handle more pressure.
  - Wood → Coal; Carbon → Diamond; Your Group → True Team.

- By its very definition, innovation is perturbation, pushing thinking and standards to new solutions.

- Being perturbed is uncomfortable, yet remembering that it's part of the path to a stronger, more stable iteration of us (self, team, or performance) is key.

- **WARNING**: The difference between pressure that traumatizes or damages people or dynamics versus pressure that can push your team to healthy greatness is the presence or lack of psychological safety in your team. If this is strong, people can and will push, take risks, and tolerate the discomfort, knowing the culture's got their back. If psychological safety is low or missing altogether, perturbation can feel hostile and dangerous.

○ A note about toxic people: If you have even one person on the team who is toxic (consistently threatening, manipulating, or undermining others), it will kill all other good work being done to unlock the team's greatness.

○ If that one toxic person is the leader, perturbation feels abusive, the negative impact is immense, and what the team can accomplish is being squashed (because people are holding back, even unconsciously, to protect themselves), although it's hard to discover.

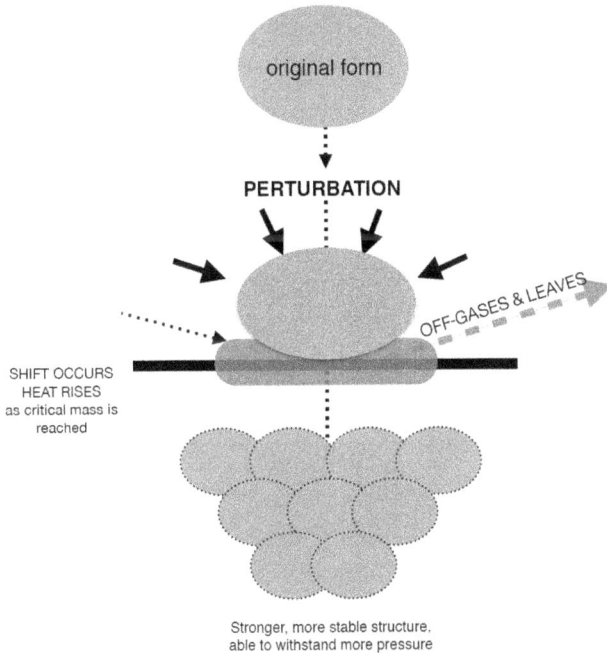

original form

PERTURBATION

OFF-GASES & LEAVES

SHIFT OCCURS
HEAT RISES
as critical mass is
reached

Stronger, more stable structure,
able to withstand more pressure

START:

- Talk with your team about where you are within the cycle of perturbation and transformation. What happens when the pressure gets hot? Do you back down to cool it off or figure out how to support one another through to the other side?

- Check in about psychological safety on the team in relation to perturbation, and get an honest assessment of its status. Frankly discuss what changes or tweaks it would take to make it psychologically safe for teammates.

- If you're the leader, take a hard look at yourself in two ways:

    1. Where you fall on the Confront-Avoid spectrum (see Chapter 4 for more details). If you're an Avoider, you may never be letting your team get uncomfortable enough to transform. If you're more of a Confronter, then ask:

    2. What are you doing to create or contaminate psychological safety and understand whether the perturbation is healthy or not? Get outside perspective on this from someone who will be honest with you, more sensitive to this than you might be, and doesn't report to you or need anything from you.

- When the team is wrestling with a tough situation or the question of "Is it worth it?" comes up, pull the diagram above out and talk through it.

- Remind one another that every pressure situation is pushing you closer to a shift; the hotter it gets, the closer you are to creating actual transformation to a stronger, more stable version of yourself or the team.

"Without trust, we don't truly collaborate; we merely coordinate or, at best, cooperate. It is trust that transforms a group of people into a team."

–Stephen Covey

17.

THE C-CHAIR OF TRUST

HOW TO QUICKLY BUILD AND REPAIR TRUST WITHOUT DRAMA

When you need this:

- All the time
- When you find yourself holding back with someone and questioning trust
- When someone questions *your* trust

Why you need this:

You feel the difference between the way you collaborate, show up, or play full out when you trust someone, vs. when you don't. Every person on your team experiences their own version of the same dynamic. Trust is fundamental for a true team and the foundation for everything you do together. That said, the words we've had to address or discuss the specificity of trust are lacking. We use generalized, blurry terms like "We have a trust issue," which doesn't easily help to get it back (What kind of trust? All of it?). You need a way to quickly get straight to what's working, what's off, and what to do to build it.

UNDERSTAND:

- We have different types of trust in play all the time.
- Each type is both easily broken and straightforwardly built or repaired. This is the **C-CHAIR** of trust:
- **C: Care.** It's personal and purposeful. Thought: Do you actually care about me — my success, me as a human being, or me as a teammate?
- **C: Confidentiality.** Privacy keeping. Thought: Do I trust that when I tell you something, you'll respect my trust by keeping it to yourself?
- **H: Honesty.** Truth-telling. Thought: Every time you tell the truth and are transparent, I trust you more. Every time you don't, or I find out that you selectively left something out of what you told me, I trust you less.
- **A: Ability.** Knowledge, skill, expertise, and experience. Thought: Do I trust that you have the skills, knowledge, or expertise to be able to do it?
- **I: Intent.** Agenda alignment. Thought: Do I trust that your intent in this conversation or engagement is pure and for the greatest good (vs. self-serving)?
- **R: Reliability.** Track record. Thought: Do I trust that your word is good? Every time you say you'll do something, then do it, I trust you more. Every time you say you'll do something, then don't do it, I trust you less.
  - Every one of the types of trust is different, though they all influence one another.

- Establishing which are solid and which are lacking allows you to reinforce how trust is happening (so it can continue) and when it's not, so you can accurately get it fixed or built.

START:

- Individually, reflect on your "trust level" with the team and individuals. Using the C-CHAIR, find specific examples of how those trust levels are solid or how they became compromised (hint: something happened). Ask the rest of the team to do the same.

- Think about what you can do to build it.

- Address individual trust issues with individual people. Before you get to which kinds of trust are lacking, first acknowledge which are solid. The conversation will flow if it starts with "I trust you in this way, this way, and this way, yet let's talk about this other way" vs. "I don't trust you," which is a process-stopper and puts the other person on the defensive immediately.

- As a team, go through the C-CHAIR as a checklist to probe each type of trust. Which are intact, and which are lacking?

- For the types of trust that are solid, point out examples of what teammates are doing that strengthen it. This helps everyone become more intentional and self-aware of their impact.

- Get clear about which type(s) of trust are lacking. *Why* are they? What is there to clean up, call out, or repair there?

- Call it, own it, recommit to what needs to change, and then move on to rebuild. (Use your new TrueTeam tools that are outlined in Chapter 3).

The CHAIR of TRUST:

C onfidentiality - do they hold the privacy of your word?

H onesty - are they telling the complete truth?

A bility - have the ability/knowledge/expertise to do what they say?

I ntent - is intent aligned with you, or do they have another agenda?

R eliability - how's their track record with you?

Each type of trust is both easily broken and straightforwardly built.

Get clear about which one is *out*... then call it, own it, recommit & move on, to rebuild.

@SSingerNourie

"Average players want to be left alone. Good players want to be coached. Great players want to be told the truth."

—Doc Rivers

18.

FEEDBACK, FOR THE WIN

HOW TO DELIVER IT, HOW TO HEAR IT

When you need this:

- You've got feedback for someone
- Someone has feedback for you
- You're considering giving feedback, yet not sure if it's worth it

Why you need this:

You know that feedback can help you and the team grow, yet giving and receiving it is tricky, which gets in the way and slows the team's learning and growth. We waste a lot of energy caught up in our heads about it — energy your team needs for more productive efforts, like actually moving forward. You need a way to give and hear feedback quickly, effectively, and frequently, without hesitation.

UNDERSTAND:

- We have a love-hate relationship with feedback:
    - We all like positive feedback.

- Most people believe that negative, redirecting, or corrective feedback is what will help them grow. Yet we don't really want to hear the negative in the moment. Statistically, according to research, people tend to prefer receiving positive feedback to the same degree that they avoid giving negative feedback!

- Most people have a harder time giving negative feedback than receiving it. (Check in with yourself about that right now.)

- The biggest challenge in hearing critical feedback is in the way it's delivered. We want to hear it, yet it's only helpful if it's given in a way we can easily hear it.

- How you tend to show up on the Avoid-Confront spectrum (see more on this in Chapter 4) shapes a lot about how you give and receive feedback. At the extremes, you might be way too confrontational for people to hear what you have to say or way too vague for people to understand the specificity of what you're saying, missing the value either way.

- Neurologically, new connections form faster in areas where there's already a connection to build on (picture new buds on an existing strong branch of a tree) than in already barren or weak areas. According to research, building on existing strengths is the fastest way for someone to learn, grow, and strengthen. The "weakness" you might be focusing on will be the hardest place for someone to have a behavioral shift. How can you capitalize on this as you deliver feedback?

- Focusing just on weaknesses shuts down learning in the brain. While we want someone to push the edges of their Comfort Zone, the fastest way is for them to step out from inside of it. If we kick them too far out of it, they go into fight/flight/freeze mode, and learning shuts down.

- You might be less open to receiving feedback than you think you are. We often say we want it (because we know we should), yet we get defensive or go below the line (see Chapter 12) in the moment, rather than actually hearing it.

- We try to "be objective" in our feedback, yet we can't, and we're confusing when we try. Saying that someone's behavior is poor as a "truth" discounts other possible perspectives, which automatically discredits your assessment because how could you possibly know all possible standards?

- The more specific and behavioral feedback is, the more effectively it can be considered and put into action.

- The way you respond when people give you feedback determines whether or not they'll give you more honest feedback going forward. If you go below the line when they give it, they'll be less likely to give it later even if they know they should. If you stay above the line, show through actions that you've listened by making some change, they'll keep being honest with you.

START:

PREP YOURSELF AS A FEEDBACK-GIVER:

- **Check your purpose.** Before you give feedback, get clear about its goal and what this person has to gain from your feedback. Make sure it's in their best interest and will move something forward for them. Think about these questions:
  - Why do you want them to hear this?
  - How is this in their best interest?

- What do they have to gain from hearing it?

- **Check your perspective.** What expertise, understanding, or vantage point do you have that they need?

PREP THE FEEDBACK:

- **Separate the behavior from the person or character.** Focus on the behavior, since we can change behavior quickly. Character or who someone is...not so much.

- **Make the behavior objective and the impact personal.** Talk about how their specific behaviors had personal impact on you and on others. This gives them an undeniable personal truth to consider (like "The whole team went from brainstorming a lot to completely silent after your comment, and we didn't really get any agreement the rest of the day"), yet it isn't an accusation or an absolute truth about them (as in "You're a jerk").

- **Build on what's there.** If you want them to effectively change or for learning to happen, link the feedback to an area where they already have strength. Building on existing strengths is the fastest way for someone to learn, grow, and strengthen.

DELIVERY:

- **Open with grounding.** Use PURPOSE + PERSPECTIVE + REASON TO CARE to give the purpose, the reason for the feedback, and your angle. For instance: "As your teammate, I know you want to be heard as an expert in this area. I have some feedback that I think will help, based on some things I'm seeing."

- Use an OITC:

  - Observation: Say what you noticed.

- ○ Impact: Here's what you can't see.
- ○ Thought: Provide an assessment.
- ○ Coaching: Try this or say "Will you please…"

HEARING FEEDBACK:

- **Choose your listening.** The only way you can hear anything valuable in anything they say is to be open to it. Consider the following:
  - ○ What do you and the feedback-giver share as priorities or commitments?
  - ○ What vantage point do they have which could be helpful?
  - ○ What expertise or experience do they have in this area?
  - ○ What's their intention in giving you this feedback?

- **Choose to be the "learner" version of yourself**, seeing the feedback-giver as the "perspective-holder." What they can see or understand about you from the outside is valuable perspective for you.

- **Acknowledge the feedback.** Say, "I heard everything you said. Thank you for that." Even better, paraphrase back what you heard to make sure you heard it all correctly.

- **Ask clarifying questions if it's not clear.**

- **Choose to accept it, or not.** If you trust their intent, care, and perspective, then take the feedback and decide how you want to take action from it (continue, begin, or change something). If you don't trust those things, either let it go, or go to Chapter 17 to learn how to have a conversation to address what's going on there.

THOUGHT: I have feedback to give!

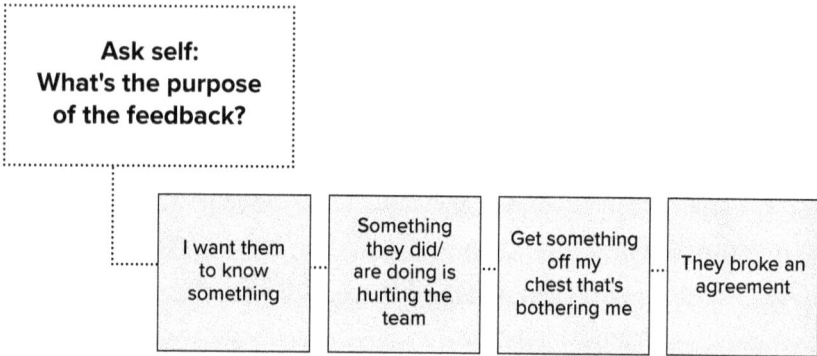

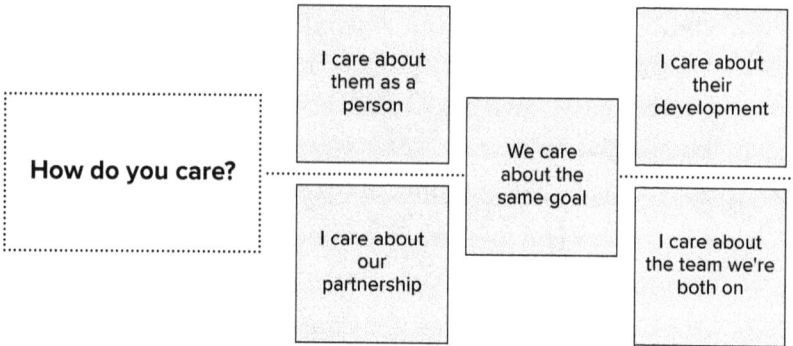

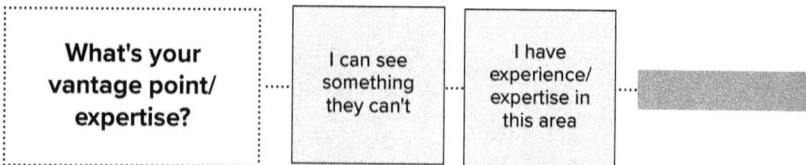

**Ask self:
What's the purpose
of the feedback?**

I want them to know something	Something they did/ are doing is hurting the team	Get something off my chest that's bothering me	They broke an agreement

How do you care?

I care about them as a person		I care about their development
	We care about the same goal	
I care about our partnership		I care about the team we're both on

What's your vantage point/ expertise?

I can see something they can't	I have experience/ expertise in this area	

Something they did/said is out of alighment with team values/ priorities	A mistake was made which needs to be corrected	You're questioning their commitment/ intention/ reliability, etc.	To put them in their place

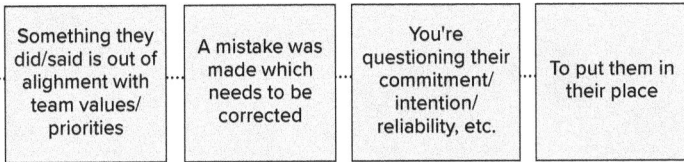

STILL IN PROCESS...

What's in it for them to hear this feedback?
What will they gain/how will they grow/why might they care?

Create:

For the sake of_____

I have feedback in the domain of

_____ to give,

based on _____.

A LITTLE ABOUT ME

Sarah Singer-Nourie coaches leaders and teams in Fortune 500 corporations, start-ups, school systems, and community organizations.

Over the last twenty years, her work has sparked breakthroughs for teams at some of America's most dynamic companies, including Target, American Eagle Outfitters, Ulta Beauty, Limited Brands, and Bubba Gump Shrimp Co. Her programs open possibility in learning and growth, creating a bridge between brain research, human performance, and real-life learning. She creates extensive training and development, from keynotes to system-wide change initiatives, specializing in leadership, learning, and teambuilding.

Sarah is the author of *Tap Into Greatness,* co-author of *Quantum Teaching,* and contributing author of *Disrupt Together.* She is the creator of the training programs *Tapping Their Greatness* and *High Impact Training & Powerful Presentations.*

Sarah has an MA in educational leadership from Saint Xavier University and a BA from The Ohio State University. She is the founder of Sarah Singer & Co., and lives in Cincinnati, Ohio, with her husband, Colin, and their three awesome kids.

For more information, visit sarahsingerandco.com.

www.ingramcontent.com/pod-product-compliance
Lightning Source LLC
Chambersburg PA
CBHW071427210326
41597CB00020B/3686